The Non-Praying Mantis

A Story about Prayer and Thankfulness

Written and Illustrated by Matt Whitlock

www.cookcommunications.com/kidz

A Faith Parenting Guide can be found on page 32.

Faith Kidz® is an imprint of Cook Communications Ministries
Colorado Springs, Colorado 80918
Cook Communications, Paris, Ontario
Kingsway Communications, Eastbourne, England

THE NON-PRAYING MANTIS
©2003 by Matthew Whitlock for text and illustrations

First printing, 2003
Printed in Singapore
1 2 3 4 5 6 7 8 9 10 Printing/Year 07 06 05 04 03

Senior Editor: Heather Gemmen
Design Manager: Jeffrey P. Barnes
Designer: Granite Design

Library of Congress Cataloging-in-Publication Data

Whitlock, Matt.
  The nonpraying mantis / by Matt Whitlock.
     p. cm.
Summary: Amanda asks her mantis family what prayer is all about, then
experiences the disappointment of praying without getting the answer she
wants, but an escape from danger helps her to understand. Includes a
"Faith Parenting Guide."
  ISBN 0-7814-3830-6
  [1. Prayer–Fiction. 2. Praying mantis–Fiction. 3. Stories in rhyme.]
  I. Title.
  PZ8.3.W594 No 2003
  [E]–dc21

                                        2002001150

Dedicated to

Amanda
and
David

Amanda was different—she'd leap and she'd play.
She didn't have time to sit down and pray.
One lovely morning she whispered to Mum,
"Why do you sit with your eyes closed and hum?"

Momma called Grandpa and Daddy came too
to tell little Mandy why they do what they do.
"We have a great God who is so full of love
we want to send praises to him high above."

We tell him we're sorry we haven't done right.
We thank him for blessings in which we delight.
We ask him for things that we want and we need.
He hears all our words and will answer indeed."

She thought to herself, "This could work well for me.
I'll ask God for friends like that cute bumblebee.
I'll ask him for muscles to make me jump higher.
I could be the girl that the kids all admire."

So the non-praying mantis pressed hands together and asked God for blessings—but didn't care whether the things that she asked for were pleasing to him. She wanted only to be filled to the brim.

She finished her prayer and stood up to jump–
but her jump was so teeny she tripped on a stump.
"What's wrong with this genie who hears all our prayers?
It seems clear to me that this God never shares.

17

"My mom and my dad,
they're too superstitious.
It's useless to pray or ask God for wishes."
She thought all these thoughts
as she went for a stroll...

then–WHOOPS!–she fell down into a big hole!

She first tried to climb out
and then screamed for help.
But she could hear nothing
except her own yelp.
"If God would have listened
and answered my prayer,
I could have jumped out
and been over there."

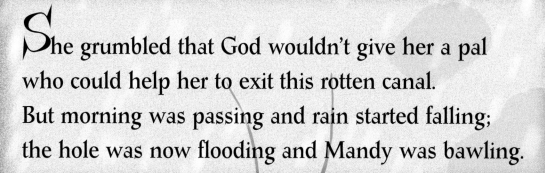

She grumbled that God wouldn't give her a pal
who could help her to exit this rotten canal.
But morning was passing and rain started falling;
the hole was now flooding and Mandy was bawling.

Oh God," she cried out, "I'm sorry for doubting.
I'm sorry for wanting so much and for pouting.
You do give me good things I need every day.
And, God, please teach me the right way to pray."

She snuffled her nose and wiped off a tear;
the raindrops stopped falling, a leaf floated near.
She climbed on the leaf, then smiled to God.
She leaped all the way from the leaf to the sod.

Just then she heard laughter high up in the sky
and a sweet buzzing voice that sounded so shy.
"I like how you jump and I like how you smile.
Is it okay if we play for awhile."

So Mandy praised God for his wisdom and grace.
She thanked him for friendship and races to race.
She never forgot her proud bug tradition:
That wonderful, humble, sweet praying position.

The Non-Praying Mantis

Ages: 4-7

Life Issue: I want my children to become people of prayer
Spiritual Building Block: Prayer

Do the following activities to help your children understand prayer:

SIGHT: Many passages in the Bible talk about prayer. Hannah prays words of praise when her request for a child has been granted (1 Samuel 2:1–10); David calls out to God for help (Psalm 77); Daniel begs God for forgiveness (Daniel 9:19); the church prays for a miracle and saves imprisoned Peter (Acts 12:5). Read these passages to your children and look for other stories that tell of people praying.

SOUND: Find a church or small group that has praying people, people who genuinely seek God. Tell your children to pay attention to how these people pray; ask them what they notice. They might notice that many of the words spoken are direct quotes from the Bible; they might notice that sometimes emotion is expressed through sighs and tears and laughter instead of words; they might notice that people of prayer pray what is pleasing to God because they are seeking his heart.

TOUCH: Remind your children to pray daily. Tell them God loves to hear them speak to him, even if their words get muddled. Teach them the A.C.T.S acronym (Adoration, Confession, Thanskgiving, Supplication) to help them stay focussed. Their daily, private prayer prepares them to pray in a group. As a family, spend time every day praying together so they can feel comfortable praying aloud and so they can hear your authentic words to God.